Master Your Focus

Focus on What Matters, Ignore the Rest, & Speed up Your Success

By I. C. Robledo
www.Amazon.com/author/icrobledo

Master Your Focus: Focus on What Matters, Ignore the Rest, & Speed up Your Success

Copyright © 2014 by Issac Robledo.

All Rights Reserved. No part of this book may be reproduced in any form without written permission from the author. Brief passages may be quoted for review purposes.

Disclaimer

Although the author and publisher have made every effort to ensure that the information in this book was correct at press time, the author and publisher do not assume and hereby disclaim any liability to any party for any loss, damage, or disruption caused by errors or omissions, whether such errors or omissions result from negligence, accident, or any other cause.

This book is not intended as a substitute for the medical advice of physicians. The reader should regularly consult a physician in matters relating to his/her health and particularly with respect to any symptoms that may require diagnosis or medical attention.

The views expressed are those of the author alone and should not be taken as expert instruction or commands. The reader is responsible for his or her own actions.

Adherence to all applicable laws and regulations, including international, federal, state, and local governing professional licensing, business practices, advertising, and all other aspects of doing business in the US, Canada, or any other jurisdiction is the sole responsibility of the purchaser or reader.

Neither the author nor the publisher assumes any responsibility or liability whatsoever on the behalf of the purchaser or reader of these materials.

Any perceived slight of any individual or organization is purely unintentional.

#10. Deal with Disruptive Ideas 38

How Can You Train Your Focus?
(Tips #11 - 18) 41

#11. Find the Sweet Spot of Challenge 42
#12. Use Brute Force Focus 44
#13. Avoid Autopilot Syndrome 47
#14. Practice Meditation 50
#15. Practice Mindfulness 52
#16. Be an Active Reader 54
#17. Play Games 56
#18. Learn Fun and Challenging Skills 58

How Can You Keep Your Focus Day After Day?
(Tips #19 - 22) 61

#19. Implement Sustainable Work Hours 62
#20. Take Smart Breaks 66
#21. Take Care of Your Body 68
#22. Make a Calming Routine 71

How Can You Get Your Whole Life into Focus?
(Tips #23 - 27) 73

#23. Find Your Internal Motivation 74
#24. Know Your Top Three Goals 76
#25. Take Stock of Big Accomplishments 77
#26. Have a Mission Statement 79

Table of Contents

An Introduction to How to Master Your Focus 1

What it Means to Lack Focus 1

Who Am I? 3

What You Will Learn from This Book 6

The Focused Mindset 8

How to Use This Book 9

Before You Continue… 11

What Should You Focus On? (Tips #1 - 4) 13

#1. Make a Schedule 14

#2. Be a Single-tasker 16

#3. Use To-do Lists 18

#4. Make Action Plans 21

What Should You Not Focus On? (Tips #5 - 10) .. 25

#5. Find a Quiet Environment 26

#6. Use the Power of 'No' 28

#7. Keep a Tidy Work Space 31

#8. Limit Your Internet Distractions 33

#9. Reduce Nonproductive Thinking 36

#27. Use Reminder Notes and Quotes 80

How Can You Make Sure You Stay Focused? (Tips #28 - 31) 83

#28. Hold Yourself Accountable 84

#29. Use a Reward System 86

#30. Seek Mentors 88

#31. Record Your Time Use 90

Final Thoughts (Tips #32 - 33) 93

#32. Stay Positive 94

#33. Practice Your Focus 95

Favorite Tips 96

A Final Reminder 97

Thank You 99

Did You Learn Something New? 100

An Invitation to the "Master Your Mind" Community (on Facebook) 101

More Books by I. C. Robledo 102

An Introduction to How to Master Your Focus

What it Means to Lack Focus

When you don't have focus, life can feel much more difficult than it needs to be. You may find that without being able to pay attention to something, you won't remember it. If you don't remember important things, it becomes even more difficult to be productive, make good choices, or even be responsible. A lack of focus can quickly make your life spiral out of control. You may miss meetings, fail an exam, or even get fired from a good job. Of course, no one wants this.

There are many reasons you may lose focus. It could be poor sleeping or eating habits. It could be a poor ability to prioritize what is important. You may not have examined your life closely enough to figure out what truly matters to you and is worth focusing on. Another issue is that you may try to take on too much in too little time. Focus has its limits. You can't force yourself to focus on everything at once. There are many more reasons you could lose your focus, more than I can list. What really matters is that whatever your reason is, it's possible to work on it and improve your focus.

I believe most people who lack focus lack it because they haven't learned the right habits necessary to build it up. If you can't focus, it's not because there is anything wrong with you. It is something that you can work on to improve if you were just shown how. You may be surprised at how much progress you can make when you learn to improve your abilities.

Who Am I?

I'm someone who has had his share of troubles with staying focused. I always thought there was something wrong with me, and that I was the only person who couldn't focus. I was completely wrong. It's a fairly common issue to have. The good thing is it can be improved. To give you an example of how bad my focus used to be, up until high school, I would sit through classes unable to pay attention. Usually I would space out and by the time I realized I had lost focus, the teacher was on another topic and I was lost. When it was time to do homework, I often had no idea where to start. I'd have to go home and try to teach myself from the textbook. It was very inefficient and I failed to improve.

In college, I decided I needed to take action to improve my focus. The classes were tougher and the professors weren't interested in hearing any excuses. If I failed to focus, I would simply flunk out. I began to experiment with my schedule, my time management, and generally pushing myself harder to stay focused. I found that I was capable of much more than I thought when I rose to the challenge. This was the point when I began discovering some of the tips which you will read about in this book.

Since my college years I've made it a daily effort to improve my focus. At one time it was difficult for me to concentrate on my work for more than a half hour at a time, but I can now go all day if I allow myself periodic short breaks.

You might think of focus as a specific muscle in your brain, a big and important one (this is just an analogy). You have to train it to improve it. Someone who wants to improve their fitness hits the gym. If you want to improve your focus, you hit the mental gym. We'll get to how you can increase your ability to focus more in the third section of this book, 'How can you train your focus?'.

I've always been interested in doing what I could to improve my mental abilities. It just so happens that focus is something that can be improved with practice. Focus is in fact one of the most important mental abilities you have. Without focus, you won't remember important things or be able to apply what you learn. Also, it can be quite frustrating to not know how to direct your focus. It can make you feel like you're on a hamster wheel running in circles. Nobody wants to be in that position.

I'd like to share a bit more of my background with you before we move on. I used to work as a researcher in a psychology lab. At the time I had to manage course work, read the latest research, conduct my own research, and write articles and book chapters. The stakes were higher there than in college. If I failed to focus I would fail myself and my lab members. I would lose a stipend and a fellowship (my source of income) as well. Ultimately, I was able to bring my focus to a higher level during my time as a researcher. Those hard-earned focus-enhancing techniques that I picked up are in this book.

I no longer work in research. I'm now an independent author. These days, I feel like I have more structure and focus in my life than if I had a 9-5 job with a boss to direct my attention. I've learned to exercise and expand my focus on a daily basis, and you can too. I don't take it for granted. My experience of needing to prioritize and direct my own focus on a regular basis has provided me with useful tips and tools you can use to improve your focus and accomplish the goals you set for yourself.

Not only do I have firsthand experience with what it's like to lack focus and with building up my focus to great levels, but I also have a master's degree in psychology. Mental abilities are something I take great pleasure from studying. The greatest pleasure of all would be to share what I know and what I've done, and for that information to benefit you. I wish to show you how to focus longer and with more clarity to accomplish your goals.

It isn't always easy or natural to stay focused on what you want to accomplish. However, I've found that with determination, and taking action to improve focus, a lot of progress can be made. Of course, a very important step is learning how to proceed to improve your focus. That's where this book comes into play.

What You Will Learn from This Book

With this book you'll be able to answer many key questions you have about focus. The questions this book answers are:

What should you focus on? Many of us would like to jump into training our ability to focus right away, but first you have to decide what is worthy of your time and energy. In this section you will decide what is most important, so you can focus most of your time and energy where it really matters.

What should you <u>not</u> focus on? Distractions are everywhere. You need a plan to cast them away so you can focus on what matters. In this section you will identify the biggest distractions in your life, and you'll make a plan for dealing with them. This way, you can invest more of your focus wisely.

How can you train your focus? There are many ways to build up your powers of focus. It's just a matter of taking the time to train. It doesn't have to be difficult or boring. This section will provide you with all kinds of ways you can start building up your focus and expanding your attention.

How can you keep your focus day after day? In order to focus for the period of a day or longer, you need to be realistic and take care of your needs. In this section, you will learn the importance of building good habits in your life so you can keep up your energy, enthusiasm, and most importantly, your focus.

MASTER YOUR FOCUS

How can you get your whole life into focus? In order to keep your focus for months or years, it helps to have an overarching focus or plan that you are working toward. In this section you'll learn ways to manage your life so that you always know what your overall purpose and goals are. This way, you'll be able to make sure your short term goals line up with your long term goals into one clear focused plan.

How can you make sure you stay in focus? You need a plan to make sure you don't fall back into old habits. In this section you can set up a system so you stay on the right track toward building your focus. It's important to monitor your progress to make sure you continue to move forward.

The Focused Mindset

Focus is a skill that you can build up. This means that your focus can be trained and improved. It's like learning anything else. If you wanted to improve at chess or at basketball, you'd practice, right? You must do the same with your focus.

Don't assume that people who can focus well were born that way. I am an example of someone who had a poor focus and was able to improve it drastically. I am now quite skilled at directing my focus where I need it to achieve my goals.

Pareto's Principle: think in terms of 80/20. This principle states that the majority of your effects (around 80%) will come from a smaller amount of causes (around 20%). What this means is that you should consider carefully where to put your focus. According to the principle, you will get most of your gains and productivity by focusing on a very few key things. Often times, we try to spread our focus into all of the dozens of things we need to do. Instead, it may be more productive to focus intently on the small part that will produce the greatest effect.

Strive for sustainable focus, not machine-like focus. It's not helpful to try to force yourself to be 100% focused all day, or for 7 days a week. In fact, it's important to take periodic breaks, and even to allow yourself to lose focus at times. Sometimes when you're losing focus, it's a signal that you need a break, to eat, or that you didn't get enough sleep the prior night. It's important not to push yourself to attain perfect focus. Instead, strive for sustainable focus. This might mean finding a plan that allows you to be at least 90% focused, 90% of the time, day after day.

How to Use This Book

This book is an organized collection of tips to focus better that have worked for me. To get the best results, you'll need to try many if not all of the tips in this book. The more tips you know, the more you can learn to combine them effectively to truly improve your overall focus. If you find that a single tip doesn't interest you, you can always move on to the next. Just make sure in the end that you have a good repertoire of tips you can use to meet your needs and improve your focus.

Most of the book follows the same structure. I define the tip, explain how it can help you focus, and list examples or a step-by-step process so you can apply what you learn. This book was specifically designed to help you take action so you can begin improving your focus right away.

Before You Continue...

As a thank you for reading, I want you to have a free guide called:

Step Up Your Learning: Free Tools to Learn Almost Anything

Have you ever wondered what the best sites and resources for learning are? It takes time and effort to figure out which sites are worth it and which are not. I hope to save you some of that time so you can spend more of it learning instead of searching the Internet.

In the past ten years or so, there has been a free learning revolution happening. More and more resources for learning are becoming available to the public at no cost. With so many new ones coming out, it's easy to miss out on some of the great learning opportunities available. Fortunately for you, this guide is short at around 4,000 words, and tells you exactly what you need to know.

The guide stems from my own experiences of using a variety of learning sites and resources. In it, you will discover the best places to go for learning at no cost. Also, I'll explain which resources are best for you, depending on your learning goals.

You can download this free guide as a PDF by typing this website into your browser: http://bit.ly/Robledo

Now, let's get back on topic.

What Should You Focus On? (Tips #1 - 4)

Without knowing what you should focus on, your energy will be spread out too thin, and you won't make as much progress as you could. This section will require you to think through what the most important parts of your days are. What deserves most of your time, energy, and focus?

#1. Make a Schedule

With a schedule you can organize important tasks into specific time slots. Usually you can use the same schedule week after week.

How this tip can help improve your focus

A schedule is good for organizing the important categories of tasks you want to focus on. When you have a schedule, your focus will improve because you'll know the important priorities you want to tackle before you even start your day.

Categories that are more important will usually get longer time slots in your schedule. If it's less important, it might get less time or you may not even put it in your schedule. Seeing this all on paper can help you remember where your priorities are.

By having your schedule laid out, you won't have to dedicate as much time to focusing on when you will do your important activities. It'll be in your schedule, so you'll already know. This allows you to put your attention completely on the tasks themselves.

How to put this tip into action

Step 1: Use Excel, Word, or paper and pencil. There may be other scheduling apps you can check out as well. I prefer to use Word for a schedule that is split into just three parts: Mon-Fri, Sat, and Sun.

MASTER YOUR FOCUS

Step 2: Decide what percentage of your time you want to be for work, chores, free time, family time, and any other important categories.

Step 3: From those percentages, figure out how many hours that translates into. You can use a calculator to multiply [percentage of time you want to spend on a task] x [available hours in your day] to get how many hours you should dedicate to a given task per day. For example, if your goal is to spend 70% of your time on work, then you'll want to figure out how many hours that is. If there are 15 waking hours you can use, then multiply that by 70% (or 0.70). You should work 10.5 hours a day in this case.

Step 4: The point is to structure your general time use — you don't need detailed categories. Broader ones are better. For example, perhaps 9-12 is office work, 12-1 is a lunch break, 1-4 is meetings, and 4-5 is email and planning. You want your schedule to help guide what you will focus on day by day.

Step 5: Fill in all of your time slots. If your Mondays to Fridays are all structured similarly, this should be fairly easy because of the repetition. If you want to maintain freedom for Saturdays, you may simply slot the whole day as a 'free day'. Make sure to leave some time for fun and relaxation in your schedule so you don't wear yourself out.

#2. Be a Single-tasker

Single-tasking is when you focus on one major task at a time, as opposed to multi-tasking where you would focus on two or more tasks at a time.

How this tip can help improve your focus

Keep in mind that focus and attention are limited resources. With a limited attention you will be more productive paying attention to one thing at a time, instead of spreading your focus thinly across different areas.

Multi-tasking can be counterproductive because it usually requires switching between two or more tasks, over and over. It's important to realize that every time you switch between tasks, you need to concentrate more to get your mind on the right track. This can exhaust your limited attention faster than is necessary.

With multi-tasking you'll need to divide your attention between different tasks. Unfortunately, you are then more likely to misunderstand something, or possibly even make a big mistake. You may not even remember what you did if you're asked later on. Multi-tasking can cause big issues because you are more likely to feel overconfident, but in reality not be well prepared at all.

Even though I've highlighted some issues with multi-tasking, it can actually work if you do it with two tasks that are simple and that you're very familiar with (you've done them hundreds of times, for example). House tasks like cleaning, cooking, and laundry are common areas where some people multi-task well. For new or complex tasks though, you're much better off focusing on one thing at a time.

How to put this tip into action

Note your multi-tasking habits. How often do you multi-task? Has it helped or hurt your productivity? Realize that productivity isn't necessarily just doing more tasks. It's also important to work on tasks that matter, and to do them well.

If you do tend to work on multiple complex tasks at a time, make an effort to focus on one task at a time in the future. This way, you'll be able to maximize your focus and perform better on one thing.

At work, you may want to divide tasks with colleagues if you can, rather than committing to doing too many things in a short time span. You can be much more productive by doing one thing right, instead of rushing several different projects with little focus on any of them.

#3. Use To-do Lists

These are simply checklists of items that you plan to do.

How this tip can help improve your focus

The great thing about to-do lists is they are an easy way to organize the things you need to get done. If organizing a to-do list sounds stressful or challenging, there are apps like Wunderlist that help make it easy. Wunderlist has many useful features to help organize and prioritize your to-do lists. As you might guess, organizing and prioritizing are fantastic ways to get yourself more focused.

As with schedules, with to-do lists you don't need to remember your items after you write them down. Instead of repeating what you need to do in your head over and over, you can relax, focus on important things, and refer to your to-do list as needed.

Another benefit of using to-do lists is that it's rewarding to check off items, motivating you to continue focusing. Many people get a good feeling to see that they've completed an important task. It's helpful to see on paper (or on an app) that you've crossed off a meaningful item. This little reward can help you stay focused and encourage you to continue to complete more items.

How to put this tip into action

You can use pencil and paper or a notepad for a daily to-do list.

There are many to-do list apps out there as well. I use Wunderlist for iPhone, a free and very helpful app. Wunderlist has many nice features, like categories of lists (work, chores, etc.), sub-lists, due dates, reminders, and flagging. Sub-lists are used to break down one item into a more detailed list. Flagging identifies your most important items.

Make your own list, and ask yourself if each task is valuable to your goals. If not, consider cutting the task. Sometimes we make our lists based on what peers are doing, what supervisors tell us, or we just do things the same way as always. These are useful strategies, but you might end up with tasks on your list that aren't very helpful or necessary. Perhaps you can cross off an item entirely, and replace it with something that takes much less time and that is more useful.

When you have your list and you're ready to get things done, start the day with the highest priority items — you'll feel better, and this makes it harder to procrastinate. Usually when I neglect to do the most important thing first, I regret it. I find it very useful to prioritize and do the most important things first. If you think about it, I'm sure you'll realize that your most important items deserve your complete focus. As the day goes on and you get more tired and new things pop up, you may find less and less time to focus on the important things, so do them first.

It's very important to keep your to-do planning all in one place. As I mentioned, I use Wunderlist to do that. I can make multiple lists with that one app. If you choose a different system, avoid having a calendar for appointments, a to-do list for your work, and other random chores on sticky notes sprawled around. This pattern can create confusion, as you have to remember which service to check for different things you need to do. Instead, merge everything into one system, and stick to it. My recommendation is to use *either* Wunderlist or Google Calendar (both free).

Another tip is if you're in a meeting, or given items to do by your supervisor, to make your to-do list immediately so you don't forget what you need to do. This is better than having to interrupt your boss or coworkers later to remind you about what you are supposed to be doing.

#4. Make Action Plans

This is a step by step plan that you can use to complete a bigger and important project. Often, when you have an item on your to-do list that you're worried about finishing on time, like 'direct film', 'write book' or 'get married', it may be time to form an action plan.

How this tip can help improve your focus

Action plans make a large task more manageable. Very large tasks can quickly become daunting and even seem frightening. To have one to-do list item that can take days or weeks is disheartening. When you find yourself in this situation, make an action plan.

When you don't know where to begin a project, it can be helpful to form an action plan as well. Writing things down often helps clarify what you need to do. This will help you stay productive by focusing on the parts of the project that matter most.

With action plans you'll be able to focus on key steps, rather than becoming distracted since it's all in front of you. With a big project it's easy to get distracted with things that are not real priorities. But if you have a clear action plan it's much easier to maintain your focus and only do what is important and necessary.

I personally find action plans to be extremely helpful. I use them regularly to guide my publishing schedule. My publishing action plan would be way too overwhelming if I didn't break it down into manageable steps. Some categories (or chunks of steps) I use are 'getting a book idea', 'crafting an outline' and 'designing a book cover'. Each of these steps can take a few days, and I further break down these categories into individual items that need to be done before the category is finished. All in all, I use a 61 step process and I make sure to cut out anything that isn't needed to meet my goal of publishing a good book. I'm happy with this action plan since it allows me to work efficiently and to stay focused. Without an action plan it could easily take a year to publish a book, but I'm able to make progress much more quickly than that.

How to put this tip into action

Step 1: Open a Word file or get a sheet of paper. I recommend using a digital file for action plans since in the end this could be a page or longer, depending on the project. You don't want to risk losing it.

Step 2: List what needs to be done to accomplish the project. At first, just make your list of what is necessary and important. You can order it when you finish.

Step 3: Categorize related chunks together. Your categories will vary drastically depending on your project, but for giving a big presentation (as an example) your categories may be: research topic, make PowerPoint slides, and rehearse presentation.

Step 4: Put 'expected time to complete' next to the categories. Aim for a week or less per category, if possible. Keep your time frames realistic. Continuing with the above example, it could take a week to research your presentation topic, two days to make slides, and another two days to rehearse.

Step 5: Review your action plan to make sure you didn't miss anything important — you may run it by a peer or supervisor. You want to be sure to include all the necessary parts you need to accomplish your project successfully.

Step 6: Also review it to make sure you didn't include anything unimportant — again, you could run it by a peer or supervisor. A common mistake is to include distractions that aren't needed for meeting your goal.

Step 7: In the end, you should have an action plan with just the key parts that need to be completed. Your timeline should be as long as it needs to be, but no longer. This way, you can focus all your attention where you need it to get the best results.

What Should You Not Focus On? (Tips #5 - 10)

Knowing what *not* to focus on, and how to accomplish that is just as important as knowing what you should focus on. We live in a world of so many distractions. Everywhere you go there is something fighting for your attention. Perhaps even now you hear people talking in the background, a television is on, and your phone alerts are updating you with pings. It's vital to learn to recognize such distractions, and to minimize them in order to put your focus where it matters.

#5. Find a Quiet Environment

You'll want to find a peaceful, quiet environment where you can concentrate without noise and interruptions.

How this tip can help improve your focus

Noise such as music, talking, or people moving around loudly can become very distracting. By having a quiet environment, you'll be able to concentrate on your goals instead of noisy distractions.

As I'm sure you know, noises can often be irritating. It's difficult to avoid getting irritated when you are interrupted over and over. Irritation, however, is just another distraction from what you're trying to accomplish. This is another reason it's important to find a quiet space to work.

By working in a quiet place you'll have less task-switching from attending to other people's conversations. When we covered single-tasking (Tip #2), you learned that when you switch tasks it takes extra time to focus again. Whether or not people have conversations with you, or between each other, it's hard not to pay attention. The best thing is to find a quiet environment to do your important work when possible.

How to put this tip into action

You may want to try out noise cancellation headphones. These are special headphones designed to counteract noise so you don't have to get distracted by your environment. They can be quite useful if you work in a noisy and distracting space.

Another useful option is to signal people as to when you shouldn't be disturbed. If you work in an office, let family or coworkers know that a closed door means you're busy, and you shouldn't be interrupted unless it's urgent.

You can also use a background noise generator like Noisli. They produce natural sounds like rainfall or crickets that can help drown out other noise and be good for focus and productivity.

As an alternative to these options, you can always play quiet music of your own to help with the noisy environment. This is only helpful of course if you can focus with your music playing. You might want to try Spotify (free on PC). Go to the 'Browse' menu, then go to 'Genres & Moods', and you can actually choose 'Focus' to find some music that may be useful.

#6. Use the Power of 'No'

'No' is a useful tool to stop yourself from doing things that aren't necessary or important to meeting your goals.

How this tip can help improve your focus

Focusing is just as much about knowing what to focus on as it is knowing what not to focus on. By saying No to distractions, lower priority items, and things that are unnecessary to your goals, you can spend more of your focus and time where it counts.

No isn't just something you say out loud, it's also a tool you can use to decide that something isn't worth the time at the moment. You may find yourself telling a coworker No when they ask you to help with a lower priority item. (You can always help them later, when you've gotten your high priority items done.) Or you may find yourself thinking No to yourself when your mind wanders to something fun you plan to do for the weekend. (You can always allow your mind to wander during a break or after work is done.)

The bottom line with No is that this tool allows you to put most of your energy into the things that really matter for your goals. It isn't negative to say or think No. It's positive because you get to highlight your priorities and focus on them instead of distractions.

How to put this tip into action

During work time, use No to stop yourself from working on anything that isn't important to your goals for the day. It's very easy to find yourself distracted. Often times we expect something to take a minute of our time, and it can easily add up to an hour or more. You're better off saying No to unimportant tasks from the start.

Use No in your reading or writing to stop yourself from wasting time on the parts that don't matter. You may usually read books and articles from beginning to end, but that could be wasteful in some cases. If you need to learn something specific, then search for the exact information you need instead of spending time reading through massive piles of information.

You can use the power of No in more unique ways too. It's actually possible to notify coworkers that you are busy working on something important without needing to tell them. You might try wearing noise cancellation headphones and putting up a sign that says 'please do not disturb when wearing headphones'. This way, you can demonstrate the power of No when distractions come to you. It's probably not wise to do this all of the time, just when you're very busy.

Another useful time to say No is when you come in contact with information that isn't actionable. If it's actionable, that means that in some way you can take action based on the information and use it to better your life or to meet some specific goal. I find it useful to ask myself if the material is actionable when choosing books or when deciding what news is worth consuming. Many books contain interesting content but they don't clearly tell you how to apply it. Of course, information can be useful without being actionable. But the busier your day is, the more crucial it is to consider if you can take action based on the information. If you can't, you may want to pass. This is why I decided to make this book as practical and immediately useful to you as I could. No matter how busy you are, you should have time for this book because it provides clear and actionable steps to improve your focus.

#7. Keep a Tidy Work Space

Make sure your work environment is generally clean and orderly.

How this tip can help improve your focus

Wasting time looking for items you need means less time to focus on your priorities. If you can't find a stapler, your sticky notes, or an important document, then your focus will already be off target. This applies not only to your physical work space, but also to files you may have on the cloud or on a drive. They should be organized enough so you won't waste time looking for what you need.

I believe that a jumbled and disorganized environment can also make for a disorderly mind. I find it difficult to prioritize what I need to do when everywhere I look I see a mess. I don't need everything to be perfectly clean, but at some point it becomes difficult to focus on anything but the mess and disorganization. I would encourage you to make it a habit to keep your work area clean and organized so it doesn't distract you from your key goals.

A dirty environment can also be a distraction. If you have old food, dusty surfaces, and excess hole punch clippings in your area, then it's probably time to clean up so you can redirect your focus back to your work.

How to put this tip into action

Routines can really help for staying clean and organized. I typically just spend a few minutes at the end of the work day making sure my office area is nice and tidy. Everything doesn't need to be perfect, but it does need to be orderly enough so I can keep my focus.

Similarly, it's a good idea to spend some time to make sure your work files (physical or digital) are organized. This could be done on a weekly basis for most purposes. The important thing is not to let it go so long that it then takes you hours of work just to get organized again.

Most people know how to clean a work space. In many buildings they will have custodial services. If your building doesn't, or if you work from home then you should do it on your own. Using cleaning wipes for surfaces and a vacuum for carpeting is a good place to start.

Another tip that may be obvious, but helpful in many cases, is to avoid eating in your office area. Eat in a lounge or cafeteria if possible. If you eat in your office area, you could get bits of food all over, and you might even attract rodents or insects. If there is nowhere else to eat, then just be sure to do a quick cleaning after you finish.

#8. Limit Your Internet Distractions

By internet distractions, I really mean any kind of technological distraction. This includes popular sites like Facebook, Twitter, and Reddit. It also includes games and apps on your phone and tablet devices as well. These kinds of sites are not bad by nature. They only become bad for you if you allow them to distract you from your key tasks.

How this tip can help improve your focus

Internet distractions are very common. These types of distractions are usually fun, engaging, and addictive. Unfortunately, that's a bad thing for keeping your focus where it needs to be.

These types of apps and programs often seem to be created as the perfect distracting systems. Your phone dings to alert you that you have a new Facebook update, or a new text or email. Twitter is designed so it's easy to get hooked and keep reading more and more, scrolling down further and further. It's important to understand the power these things have, so you can learn to manage them and keep your focus.

Another thing to realize is that the *more* time you invest into these things, the *more* you tend to get hooked and want to spend even *more* time on them. These programs are often designed to reward you for using them. For example, it can feel good to collect followers or friends, which encourages you to spend your limited time on such programs. Unfortunately, it's easy to enter into an unhealthy cycle of use that's difficult to break.

Of course, it's important to make sure you don't get sucked into these kinds of addicting distracters, especially when you have more important things to do. I use plenty of these sites and I enjoy them, but I limit my time with them to make sure they don't become a distraction from my goals.

How to put this tip into action

One good thing to do is to identify your biggest distracters. Do you find it difficult to stay away from a game on your smart phone, a social media page, or any other apps? If you have specific distracters that repeatedly call for your attention, it's important to identify them first so you can find a way to stop them.

It may be a good idea to stop notifications on your phone for these big distracters. A smartphone can be very distracting if it has alerts with all kinds of sounds going off every few minutes. Simply turning off the alerts can really help. Go to your smartphone settings or contact customer support to stop unwanted alerts.

Another way to help your productivity and focus is to choose only certain hours of the day to engage in your top distracters. Perhaps you can live with only checking your Facebook page after 5PM, for example. I avoid checking any social sites until after 5PM to keep up my focus and productivity. I find this really helps.

I prefer to be fairly strict when it comes to email since it can become a huge distraction. Usually the less amount of times you allow yourself to check your email, the more it will help your focus and productivity. If you can create three email checkpoints for yourself, this should be a great improvement over the 10+ times most people check their email. I usually check mine at 9 a.m., 1 p.m., and 5 p.m. Even though I check mine in the morning, I won't spend more than five to ten minutes on it. It's important not to get too distracted with emails. Remember your priorities and focus on that instead. Timothy Ferris wrote a blog post about his experience with only checking his email twice a day, if you're interested in trying that – it's titled *How to Check E-mail Twice a Day… And Have Your Boss Accept It*.

You might find it helpful to occasionally take a fast from your big distracters, perhaps even from internet services altogether. It doesn't need to be for a full day. A good time to do this might be weekdays an hour before you generally go to bed. This sort of routine can help you pull away from the *need* to engage with these popular apps and sites. If you train yourself to want them less in your free time, you'll be able to want them less during your work time.

I know many websites can be huge distracters for some people. For you it may be one of the ones I already mentioned, or it could be something else. If you have a serious issue stopping yourself, it could be worth looking into websites/apps that help you block sites for time periods that you choose. For example, FocalFilter (for Windows) provides this service.

#9. Reduce Nonproductive Thinking

Nonproductive thinking is any thought that distracts you from your goals. Distractions come not only from our environment, but they can also come from our own minds.

How this tip can help improve your focus

When you pay attention to new, irrelevant, or destructive thoughts coming in, you lose your focus on what you're trying to accomplish. Unfortunately, these kinds of thoughts can put your focus on doubts about yourself and your abilities, rather than getting things done. If you learn to redirect your focus outward to your task, you can help keep your focus better.

By reducing or eliminating these nonproductive thoughts, you can put more energy into your true goals.

How to put this tip into action

First, realize that you can reduce your nonproductive thoughts if you work on them, but eliminating them isn't a realistic goal.

When you have negative thoughts about your ability to perform your work, or something in your home life, it can help to redirect your mind. Instead of focusing on the problems themselves, think about what actions you can take to improve the situation.

If your thoughts often get in the way of your progress, try to focus outward to the task that you want to complete. A tip given to people who want to improve their public speaking for example, is to focus on what they want to teach to the audience. To focus on worrying thoughts about what people think will only make performing any task more difficult. It's better to redirect your focus to the task itself.

Avoid nonproductive thinking from others. Examples of this may be workers who spend a lot of time on gossip, or people who always talk about and expect the worst to happen.

Meditation (discussed further in Tip #14) is an activity that can help with gaining control of your thoughts. With some meditative techniques, you train yourself to see your thoughts neutrally, and recognize that they are not a true assessment of reality. By seeing your thoughts as an objective observer, you're better able to see the situation for what it is, rather than assuming that your thoughts are always an accurate reflection of reality. This may be confusing, but it's easier to understand if you learn more about meditation and practice it. Any beginner book should be useful for this.

#10. Deal with Disruptive Ideas

These are any ideas coming from you or elsewhere that distract you from your goals. They can be ideas that seem brilliant at first, but often turn out to be impractical. They can also be work interruptions, such as coworkers asking for help or favors.

Disruptive ideas are different than nonproductive thinking (Tip #9) because sometimes these ideas can actually be productive later on. A disruptive idea might be something creative that could possibly be put to use later.

How this tip can help improve your focus

New ideas that don't fit into your daily plan will disrupt your goals for the day. Any time someone comes to you with a new idea, or you come up with an idea doesn't fit into your goals, it will disrupt your focus. Even if the idea does fit into your goals, but the time isn't right for it, it can still disrupt your focus. For this reason we need a plan to deal with disruptive ideas.

A rule to keep in mind with new ideas is that if it isn't urgent, then it's a distraction. Obviously, if there is something that needs immediate attention, then you should take care of it. But if you can, you should put the disruptive idea aside and maintain focus on your goals.

For example, sometimes when I'm working I'll come up with a random question that has nothing to do with my work. The question could be 'how many dimensions are physicists aware of?' When that happens, I'll write the question down to get it out of my mind and continue with my work. Later on when I've completed my priorities I'll look up the answer to my question if I still want to know.

How to put this tip into action

Step 1: You get a disruptive idea, or a disruptive idea is brought to your attention.

Step 2: If it's urgent, do it right away.

Step 3: If it's somewhat important and it can be done quickly (in a few minutes), do it right away.

Step 4: Otherwise, take out a notebook, use Evernote, a voice recording app, or sticky notes.

Step 5: Write down or record the disruptive idea and put it aside. (Don't evaluate it, research it, or think about it. You've already decided that it wasn't important enough for that.)

Step 6: Later on when your priority tasks are done for the day, you can decide if the idea is important enough to put on your to-do list.

How Can You Train Your Focus? (Tips #11 - 18)

This section is probably the reason you chose to read this book. I hope by now you realize that knowing what to focus on, and what *not* to focus on is critically important. Without having mastered these concepts, training to improve your focus will be of limited use. If you don't have a strategy for what to focus on and for avoiding distractions, I'd urge you to read those parts first.

#11. Find the Sweet Spot of Challenge

This is when you find just the right amount of challenge you need in your day to help bring out your inner focus.

How this tip can help improve your focus

Think about it. If something isn't challenging enough, you'll get bored and lose focus. If something is too challenging, you won't be able to maintain your focus or be productive because the task is too difficult for your ability. What you want is the sweet spot of challenge, where you're forced to focus to keep up with the challenge.

Personally, I've found that when I give myself a challenging but achievable task, I end up focusing more to keep up with the challenge, and I end up getting more done as a result. Finding the appropriate level of challenge for yourself can take some trial and error, but it is well worth it when you find your ability to focus leaps forward.

How to put this tip into action

Realize that you are probably capable of much more than you think you are. For example, I used to write 2,000 words a day. At the time, that seemed like a decent challenge. However, I found that when I raised the stakes to 3,000 I was still able to accomplish the task. Then I raised it to 4,000, which required even more focus, but I could still do it. I don't believe the quality has gone down because my focus tends to go up with the level of challenge. I know I can still do more. I haven't reached my limits yet.

A good way to apply the sweet spot of challenge to your life is to try to take on just a bit more than you think you can really handle. Or try to take on just one step above what you normally do. By taking on a bit more, you'll get yourself closer to that sweet spot. You'll know when you're at or near the sweet spot, because you'll feel more intensely focused on your task. Outside distractions will tend to melt into the background. You won't feel flustered (if you do, you may have pushed too hard), but you will feel engaged. Time may appear to speed up or slow down — this is normal when you're extremely focused. And of course, at the end of the day you'll have been more productive than usual. You may even surprise yourself.

#12. Use Brute Force Focus

This is a technique where you focus intently on a highly challenging task for as long as it takes to complete it.

How this tip can help improve your focus

This technique forces you to expand your ability to focus. By engaging intently on a very challenging task, you will train yourself to stretch your focus, improving your ability to think intensely about one problem for long periods.

Brute Force Focus is one of the most useful techniques there is to improve your focus. The benefit is that you train your focus on the specific tasks that are important to you. You build your ability to focus, and you build your ability to solve challenging problems that matter to you.

One reason this technique can help build focus is because you aren't supposed to back down from the task even as distractions or obstacles arise. With this technique you enter a mental space where only you and the problem in front of you exist. Everything else is just irrelevant noise. With this attitude and approach you can build up your ability to focus longer and more intensely.

In college I ended up discovering this Brute Force Focus technique as a matter of necessity. I enrolled in an extremely difficult chemistry class and I quickly discovered I was in over my head. I had failed the first homework assignment, and I frequently felt lost during the professor's lectures. As the weeks passed, the homework became even tougher and tougher. There were often thirty questions, and many of those questions had ten parts that needed to all be answered perfectly. There was no credit for a partially correct response. This meant if I got 9 parts correct out of a 10 part question, I still got the question wrong.

I ended up using Brute Force Focus to stay up late at night working on the homework. It wasn't easy at all. A lot of the time I wanted to quit and relax, but I forced myself to keep focusing and working because I wanted to perform well. I would spend hours sometimes just making sure I did one problem correctly. This might seem silly, but trust me these problems were tough and tricky. Ultimately, in the end 75% of the class had dropped the course or failed. A close friend of mine who was quite smart confided in me that he earned a D, and that he'd be retaking the course. I was on the line somewhere between a B and an A, and the professor gave me the A. Sometimes when you really want to succeed, you're not left with a better option than to brute force it.

How to put this tip into action

Step 1: Adopt a 'won't give up no matter what' attitude. The stakes should ideally be low or moderate, but imagine that they are higher, that people are counting on you to get this task done.

Step 2: Choose a very challenging task. Of course, this task should be something that isn't likely to cause irreparable harm if you were to make a mistake.

Step 3: The task should be possible to accomplish, but difficult enough that you're not sure if you will succeed.

Step 4: Ideally, the task should be possible to complete within about 30 minutes to 2 hours.

Step 5: Focus on your one task 100% until you accomplish it.

Step 6: Obstacles will likely arise, but you must persist in looking for solutions to them as they come up. Use everything you know, and only seek outside resources as a last resort.

(*Step 7*: It's okay to stop at some point, as long as you stretch your focus rather than give up too easily.)

#13. Avoid Autopilot Syndrome

Autopilot syndrome is when we jump into routines with no real thought. This can happen with tasks that we do all the time. The task becomes automatic and we tend to underestimate the dangers or problems that can arise.

How this tip can help improve your focus

Autopilot syndrome can create bad focus habits because you simply expect patterns to hold as they always do, rather than focusing on what is in front of you. Focus requires consciously controlling your attention, whereas autopiloting allows unconscious or routine processes to take over.

When we get used to autopiloting, our ability to focus can decrease because we aren't exercising our focus enough. It's easier to be on autopilot, but it isn't helpful for developing our mental abilities. Without pushing yourself mentally, your abilities will decline.

Actively fighting autopilot can help rebuild focus. By fighting it, you redirect your mind to focusing on what is actually happening, rather than assuming that everything will be the same as always. The bottom line is that to train your focus, you have to actually focus. If a large part of your day is taken over by routine tasks, it's especially important to practice your focus and keep your mind in top shape.

The more potentially dangerous a task is that you wish to complete, the more crucial it will be for you to avoid autopilot syndrome. For example, it seems appropriate to consider the job of a pilot. With so many modern technological features on commercial planes, they can keep the plane on autopilot for most of the flight. However, they must stay focused and keep reading the gauges to make sure that no problems arise. If pilots allow themselves to lose focus and rely too much on automatic systems, the results can be disastrous, costing many lives.

Make sure to be especially cautious when working on tasks that could be dangerous. Avoid autopilot syndrome to help prevent disasters. Of course, by training yourself to avoid this syndrome you can improve your focus as you train to keep your mind stimulated.

How to put this tip into action

Identify common autopiloting tasks you engage in. You may work in a job that involves a lot of routine. Perhaps you spend hours passively watching television. Maybe you drive every day while putting little thought into it. The first step is to identify these kinds of tasks. The more of your day they take up, the more important it is to monitor them.

If you find that such routine tasks take up a lot of your day, perhaps more than just a few hours, then it's important to eliminate or reduce them. Of course, you can't always do this. Perhaps a good portion of your job involves routine tasks where you tend to autopilot.

Another way to tackle autopilot syndrome besides eliminating the tasks is to find a way to make the tasks less routine. You may add novelty, create a game (even if it's just in your mind), or create a new challenge for yourself. The important thing is to find a way to change the task from a routine, to something new that you need to focus on.

An interesting thing to do is simply to challenge yourself to perform better at everything you do, no matter how trivial or routine the task seems. For example, when driving you can make a special effort to always stay in your lane, to obey speed limits, use turn signals, and make complete stops at stop signs. If these become routine and trivial, you can add novelty by attempting to create meaning out of people's random license plate numbers.

Sometimes driving through my town I'll find myself going on autopilot because I usually take the same roads to the same places. An easy way to kick your mind back in gear is to try a new route. Even changing one minor thing like taking a new road can get your focus back on task. Of course, you can use this principle with other areas of your life to regain focus too.

#14. Practice Meditation

Meditation is an ancient spiritual practice, originating in Eastern cultures. In modern times it has become popular in the West, where it's often used for relaxation purposes.

How this tip can help improve your focus

Meditation isn't just for relaxation. It's a great way to help clear your mind too. The average person now has so many different worries and issues to deal with that meditation can be useful to help free your mind from distraction. With your mind cleared up, you'll be able to choose what truly deserves your focus with a fresh start.

Meditation also helps to train you to direct your mind and focus intently on one thing. With practice it's possible to improve and direct your focus more and more intensely. The powers of focus I find in meditation are stronger than any normal focus I usually attain in my waking life. Of course, while meditating you aren't accomplishing goals directly, but it is still useful for training the mind.

A very important part of the meditative practice is that it trains you to redirect your mind back to your task when you lose focus. Often times in our daily lives, it's easy to get distracted by Twitter or email, and we use websites where one link takes us to the next, and the next, and so forth. We allow ourselves to be distracted, rather than putting a stop to it. Meditation specifically trains redirecting focus back on the goal, back where it matters. It doesn't encourage or reward becoming distracted.

How to put this tip into action

Keep in mind that the following steps are only for one kind of meditation that I find useful:

Step 1: Find a quiet room where you won't be disrupted. Dim or turn off the lights.

Step 2: Get in a comfortable position. Sitting in a recliner leaning back is what often works for me. However, you don't want to be so comfortable that you fall asleep.

Step 3: Take deep, slow breaths, and focus on your breathing completely. Repeat this over and over.

Step 4: When distracting thoughts creep in, gently guide your attention back to your breathing. When you get distracted don't feel that you've failed. This is a normal part of the process, and the important thing is to redirect your attention back to your breathing, calmly.

It can be helpful to start with 5 minute sessions and to gradually move up in 5 minute increments to help improve your focus.

#15. Practice Mindfulness

Mindfulness is about being in the moment. It's about allowing yourself to be present so you can fully enjoy and comprehend the moment. With mindfulness, you put aside concerns about other things. The goal is to completely immerse yourself in the immediate task or environment.

How this tip can help improve your focus

Mindfulness trains you to hold your attention on one thing longer. With this technique you make a conscious effort to keep your focus. That effort trains you to use your focus more deliberately, more consciously.

By practicing mindfulness you can learn to focus more deeply and intensely. You put all of your focus into what is happening immediately. It helps you learn to allow in less intrusive thoughts about problems in the past, or worries about the future. This gives you more mental energy to focus with. With this training you can become better at avoiding distracting thoughts, because the goal is to center your attention on the present.

How to put this tip into action

With mindfulness, I recommend you use the same technique mentioned with meditation (Tip #14). When you practice the technique, every time you find yourself becoming distracted, redirect your attention back to the present. This simple act helps to train you to maintain your focus better.

MASTER YOUR FOCUS

There are many ways to practice mindfulness. I'll mention some that you may find helpful.

A mindful walk is a nice way to practice this skill. You simply go for a walk and focus on the environment. Push your daily concerns aside and enjoy your surroundings and any plant or animal life in the area.

Having a mindful conversation is another thing you can try. How often do you speak with people without really paying attention to what they're saying? You might think too much about what you want to say instead of listening. Or you might be playing with your phone while they talk. Instead, practice having a mindful conversation. To do this, you should stop anything else you were doing and genuinely and thoughtfully engage in a discussion with someone. Pay attention to facial expressions, tone of voice, and the message they want to tell you.

You can even practice mindful eating. We often eat when distracted with work, when in a rush to do something else, or when watching television. Once in a while try eating your food and paying attention to the flavor, the smell, and how satisfying the meal is.

There is another mindfulness technique that can be quite fun as well. You can try listening to music, paying attention to all the instruments, all the singers, all the beats and rhythms and subtleties of the song. It can be quite entrancing and relaxing to do this with many kinds of music.

#16. Be an Active Reader

Active reading involves building your attention and learning what to focus on through reading exercises.

How this tip can help improve your focus

Reading is such a huge part of most of our lives that it makes sense to practice improving your focus on what you read. This is especially true if you often notice your focus drifting away as you read. With active reading, you will learn to pay attention to what you read for a longer period. You'll be able to focus more on the parts of the book that matter most, and disregard the parts that aren't relevant. It's important to know what to focus on when reading to avoid wasting time and energy.

With active reading you can learn to understand more of what you read with less effort. Books can take a long while to read, so it's important to use your focus efficiently. Remember, focus is a limited resource.

How to put this tip into action

Try using the SQ3R method. It stands for survey, question, read, recite, and review. First, survey the book. Read through the back of the book description, look at the table of contents, and review book chapter headings. Then form questions for every section of the book. Next, read the book and find the answers to the questions you had. After this, you should recite, or remember those answers. Finally, at a later time you should review to make sure you still remember the answers to the questions. Those answers should be the main points of the book that were most important for you to know. For more detail on SQ3R you can go to http://www.studygs.net/texred2.htm

This method really helps highlight your focus so you get more out of what you read. Without purpose or focus when you read, it's easy to plow through tens or hundreds of pages and find at the end that you learned or understood very little. You may not even know where to begin to apply the information.

In addition to the SQ3R method, it can be useful to practice reading more incrementally. You may have noticed by now that I like the idea of increasing the level of challenge gradually. I believe strongly that adding on challenges bit by bit can help you improve your abilities. To practice reading more incrementally, you might try reading 10 pages one night, 15 pages the next, 20 pages the next, and so forth. You can practice the meditative technique of bringing your focus back to the page if you get distracted.

Another way to train your reading and to improve your focus is to practice reading more challenging books. You can gauge how difficult a book is by reading the description online, or reading the back side of its paper copy. It may also help to read some reviews. In general, some easier genres will be self-help, how to books, and young adult fiction. More challenging genres would be philosophy, science, and futuristic sci-fi. Of course, there is wide variation in difficulty within genres. If you want an extra challenge, academic textbooks and articles tend to be more challenging. Also, old classical texts like Homer's *The Odyssey* or Shakespeare's plays, or other books between those time periods (around 1600 and earlier), will usually be more challenging.

#17. Play Games

There are different kinds of games that can be useful for improving focus. Board games like Chess and Go require a lot of concentration to be able to play them. There are also games that were specifically designed for improving focus (or attention), such as those found at Lumosity or Cambridge Brain Sciences.

How this tip can help improve your focus

Chess and Go are unique games, but they are similar in that they have simple rules that allow for a great deal of complexity to arise. In the first few moves of a chess game there are millions of possible positions. With Go you can actually arrive at even more positions. Because these games offer so many possibilities, the players must focus in order to have a chance to win.

Just learning how to play these games competently takes focus. There are all kinds of strategies that can be used, so the beginner has to pay close attention to learn the game at a level where they have any chance of winning.

It also takes a great level of sustained focus to play these games well. With either of these games, one poorly thought out move can end in immediate defeat. If you want to compete and win, a great deal of focus is needed.

MASTER YOUR FOCUS

How to put this tip into action

It doesn't take very long to learn to play Chess or Go. The rules are quite straightforward and it's easy to jump online and start playing real people in a matter of minutes. Chess Tempo (http://chesstempo.com/) is also a good site where you can improve your focus by solving challenging chess problems. You might be interested in trying it if you're already familiar with the game.

Of course, these games aren't for everyone. If you're looking for something that is more immediately fun and doesn't require you to learn specific rules, you may want to try sites that help train your focus directly. Some sites have games for this, like Lumosity (free trial) and Cambridge Brain Sciences (free). Try games that are meant to improve focus, attention, or concentration.

The argument could be made that all kinds of games may be useful for improving your focus. Many video games, for example, are quite complex and require a lot of skill and attention to perform well. If you want to try improving your focus by playing games, I would recommend trying some that are new to you. To get started you can type "free games" into your search engine. If you're looking for something more, you can always look up console or PC games.

I should mention that it's easy to get distracted with games. I wouldn't recommend getting too carried away with them. Set limits on how long you will play, or only play them on days when you don't have work.

#18. Learn Fun and Challenging Skills

Learn skills that are a challenge to learn, but not so challenging that they frustrate you. Also, try to learn skills that you will enjoy practicing.

How this tip can help improve your focus

A great way to improve your focus is to learn fun and challenging skills. It takes a lot of time, effort, and focus to improve at a new skill. You will need to focus just to learn and make progress. For this reason, learning something new will be good for drawing out your focus.

It's important to choose a skill that is just the right level of challenge. That way, you'll need to continue to focus even as you learn and improve. The great benefit of learning a new skill is that it's good for your focus, but of course you will also learn something new which should be useful.

How to put this tip into action

There are plenty of skills that are challenging for most people that you could learn.

You could try to learn a new sport like tennis. When you are new to a game, it can be an extra challenge to become good. It's important to find a coach or partner that can help teach you what to focus on as you learn.

Another skill that is often challenging to learn is a musical instrument like piano. With piano, you have to learn to read music, where your hands are supposed to go, and how to use the pedals. Playing piano music is simple in that it's mostly a matter of hitting the right keys, but learning to do this effectively requires great focus and practice. Early on, one of the more challenging things to learn is to play with both hands simultaneously, as they both play different rhythms. I've played piano and observed people learning, and I believe that it is a higher level challenge, but it can be very fun and rewarding.

You could also try learning a language. There are apps that make it easy to begin learning. You may want to try Duolingo (available on the web/iOS/android), as they make it fun and easy to get started. I've used the app to learn some basic words in German.

Yoga is also a skill that can take focus and practice to perform well. You would probably want to find a class in your town or look up instructional videos if you want to pursue this.

Surely, there are many other skills to try. If it's challenging and it draws out your focus and you're engaged, that's all you need to help train your focus. Find something interesting to you, and commit to it. Don't allow yourself to give up within a month. Fight through the challenge and expand your focus.

How Can You Keep Your Focus Day After Day? (Tips #19 - 22)

Now that you've read through the sections dealing with what to focus on, what not to focus on, and how to train your focus, we can discuss important things you can do to extend your focus even longer. This section will cover what you can do to make sure you stay focused all day, day after day. This is an important section because most people want to stay focused on the job or for some other important project that takes real time and effort. Focusing isn't a sprint where you do it for an intense burst and you're done. It's more of a marathon where you want to ensure that you can keep going even on the tough days. These tips will show you how.

#19. Implement Sustainable Work Hours

Sustainable work hours are when you schedule your work in a way that you can keep your energy, motivation, and focus stable and high through the whole day.

How this tip can help improve your focus

A binge work session would be a good example of *not* using sustainable work hours. If you find yourself studying until five in the morning, or working all day at the office and then going home to answer emails and do extra work at home until midnight, then these are the kind of binges that are not sustainable. Sooner or later, working in binges will drain you. It depletes your energy, your focus, and your ability to understand and learn new information.

Working sustainably will involve paying attention to your needs. If you're exhausted, it's all the more important to get proper rest so you can come back and focus the next day. It's about finding a routine that works for you to optimize your focus day after day.

Remember that we are not perfect focusing machines. It's unrealistic to expect yourself to be able to focus at 100% all day. Even focusing 100% for an hour is quite a stretch for many people. If you space out for a minute here and there, you shouldn't let it bother you too much. The important thing is to have a routine that enables you to focus longer and more intensely, for days, weeks, even months at a time without burning out. That's my goal, not 100% focus.

How to put this tip into action

The Pomodoro technique can be quite helpful for guiding your focus in a sustainable way. There are different variations on this technique. I prefer to use the one where you focus intensely on one thing for 25 minutes, then take a 5 minute break, and repeat. In an office environment, you might consider trying 55 minutes of work and then taking a 5 minute break. You could tell your supervisor that this helps improve your focus and productivity. I can't guarantee you'll be allowed to do it, but it might work (besides, you could turn that into a tea break or a bathroom break, which may be more accepted).

I enjoy using this method for activities that require a great deal of concentration. It's much more manageable to set a goal to focus intensely for 25 minutes, than it is to focus intensely from 9-5. There is a free app called 30/30 (on iPad and iPhone) that is quite useful for making this all automatic. I use it regularly. It takes a bit of playing around with to set up, but you may find it helpful.

Another tip to create a sustainable focus routine is to spread out your work. If you know Mondays are super busy, then make an effort to tackle some of that workload on other days. I find that it helps to have a fairly even workload from day to day. Uneven workloads can't always be avoided, but if you think about it you may find that there are ways to split up important tasks and still get them done on time.

It's also important to plan ahead. Don't allow yourself to get ambushed into doing 15 hours of work in one day because you didn't plan ahead. If you have a wildly hectic work life, you should consider planning your weeks in advance to avoid big surprises. Sunday night is a good time to do this.

If you want to sustain your focus, you'll want to get your procrastination in check. We all do it. I can hardly think of anyone I know that never procrastinates. The horrible thing about procrastination is you often end up piling up important tasks that need to get done. A good way to avoid this is to commit every day to doing the most important tasks first. That way you work and focus harder at the beginning of the day, when people usually have more energy. This improves your ability to sustain your focus through the day, as your tasks will get easier (if you got the hard ones out of the way).

Another very useful tip is to set work time boundaries. When you have a lot of work, or big ambitions, you may be tempted to work all the time. It seems logical, but really this is often counterproductive. The reason is working nonstop is not sustainable. If you have a lot of energy, you might last a week or even a month, but then you'll probably collapse and burnout. You're better off setting limits on when you will not work. My setup is I won't work after around 7PM on weekdays or Sundays, and Saturdays I take the day off. If you can, I would encourage you to take at least one day off so you can get away from 'work mode' and recharge your focus. Doing so will give you time off to rest and come back stronger. It also forces you to organize your time and to focus intensely when you are working. Without work time boundaries, sometimes we can get into a pattern of working nonstop, but with poor focus. This is a bad habit you'll want to avoid.

#20. Take Smart Breaks

Smart breaks are when you optimize your break patterns. Taking breaks when you need them will allow you to keep your energy and efficiency high through the day.

How this tip can help improve your focus

Sometimes you need to rest so you can come back to your work refreshed and focused. I think of focus as a gasoline meter in your car. If you get down to 0 gas, you can sit there and try to keep cranking the engine, or you can refuel the car so it can actually run. It's the same with your focus. When you're near the end of your abilities, it might make more sense to regenerate your focus by giving it a rest than to keep trying to push forward when your body doesn't want to.

How to put this tip into action

When you find yourself exhausted, constantly day dreaming, and losing focus, allow yourself a short break to get re-energized. There's a point where pushing yourself to keep going will just frustrate you more and burn up what little focus is left.

On your short breaks, do something completely different. If you spend most of the day staring at a screen, get up and move around. Do some jumping jacks, sit ups, or push-ups. If you do a lot of physical activity, then find a comfortable chair if you can and relax your muscles for a bit.

MASTER YOUR FOCUS

I'll mention the Pomodoro technique again. That system has built in breaks, so it's a 'set it and forget it' sort of thing. If you can build in periodic breaks into your day automatically, you'll be better off because you won't have to think about whether or not you feel like you need a break. Again, the 30/30 app can be useful for this.

Smart breaks are 'smart' because you have to judge what kind of break you need, and how long it should be. If you've been on a work binge (even though it's not recommended in Tip #19) then perhaps you need more than just a short break. It may be a good idea to give yourself a much longer break if possible. For example, you could watch simple TV programs for an hour, or you could go to sleep for the night.

#21. Take Care of Your Body

This means eating healthy foods, exercising, and sleeping well to keep your energy and focus high.

How this tip can help improve your focus

Your focus depends largely on your body's energy levels. And your energy then depends on how well you take care of your body. So if your body isn't well taken care of, this is going to deplete your energy levels. That means you'll have less energy to focus with. Your body will be using most of that limited energy just to keep from falling asleep. That's bad for productivity.

Another issue with not taking good care of your body is that you'll have problems focusing because your mind will be more concerned with your body. For example, if you didn't sleep well, your mind will drift to wanting sleep. If you didn't eat well, your mind will drift to wanting food. If you didn't exercise, your mind might drift to your cramping muscles. These are big unnecessary distractions that will kill your focus.

If you allow your body to be in bad care, it will certainly poison your ability to focus. Taking care of yourself is important for maintaining an optimal level of focus. Of course, it's generally good for your health and wellbeing anyway.

A couple of years ago I actually developed a mild case of hypoglycemia (low blood sugar) from trying to push my focus too far. I worked too long, exercised too little, and I wasn't eating enough to keep my energy up. This schedule took a toll on my focus as I lost energy and felt weak regularly. My doctor told me to eat more often to stabilize my blood sugar. I followed his advice, but it took about a year of carefully watching my diet and exercising to completely eliminate my symptoms (low energy, tiredness, etc.). I mention this as a warning to you. It's much easier to take care of your body regularly than to have to repair things when they go completely wrong. Your body is kind of like a car in that way, where regular maintenance is the way to go. Wanting to improve your focus is great, but you have to know your limits and take care of your bodily needs.

How to put this tip into action

As part of my routine, I'll eat three nutritious meals a day with a small snack in between big meals to keep my blood sugar stable. It's difficult to give detailed advice to you, since people of different sizes, ages, and genders have different needs. What I do recommend is experimenting to find a setup that allows you to feel more energetic and focused through the day. However, if your eating habits aren't good enough to maintain your energy, then it may help to see a dietitian to get back on track.

Personally, I avoid consuming too much caffeine, sugar, and alcohol. Too much caffeine can make it difficult to sleep, although some caffeine can help with focus. Too much sugar is generally not good for your body or energy. It can spike your blood sugar, leading to an energy crash. This sort of thing isn't good for your focus. Remember, we want routines that enable us to sustain our focus day after day, not just for a short burst. And as far as alcohol is concerned, we all know that too much of it isn't good for our focus.

It's a great idea to make sure you move your body every day. When your body is well taken care of, your mind will be able to stay better focused. Unfortunately, a lot of us are getting less and less exercise. Why not simplify the goal to just getting some kind of movement? Take the stairs at your work, go for a 5 minute walk daily, do jumping jacks, or ride your bike. If you can, you may want to organize a game of tennis or ping pong once a week with a friend. Start small and simple.

Get your sleep schedule regulated by sleeping at the same time every night. This one tip has done wonders for me. Preferably, go to sleep before midnight. Our ancestors went to sleep and got up with the sun. It makes sense that to deviate wildly from this could put us out of sync with our natural systems. Having a routine sleep pattern will help you make sure you get up when you want and that you feel energized at the start of your day. Again, your energy will affect your focus, so it's important to keep it high and stable. Start with a good night's rest.

Monitor your energy levels. Poor energy means poor focus. Who wants to be unenergetic anyway? Occasionally throughout your day, ask yourself, how energized do I feel? Am I dragging my feet, or am I happy, motivated, and full of energy to keep going? If at any point you feel that your energy is off, it's likely to be a problem with your sleep, your eating, or your activity levels. Experiment and try to figure it out.

#22. Make a Calming Routine

This is a specially designed routine just for you. The purpose is to help calm you down on an extra stressful day. You can also use similar routines for when you feel overworked, drained, and burnt out.

How this tip can help improve your focus

Everyone has days that are super stressful, but there is so much work to be done that there is no time to even stress out. Perhaps you need to finish a massive pile of work by the deadline, which just so happens to be tomorrow.

A calming routine is exactly what you need when this happens. It takes little time, only 5 minutes. Ideally, you could take the day off of work and go straight to the sauna, but if you could do that then it wouldn't be much of a stressful day, would it?

Stress brings about an unfocused chaos from inside of you. When you're really stressed, your mind stops working properly. Your focus becomes difficult to manage, as your mind races all over the place. A calming routine will help you get your mind relaxed and back in order.

How to put this tip into action

Think about tasks that can help you get your mind off of work and also soothe your mind. It helps if you can think of anything in the past that has helped you calm down in a tough situation. Or perhaps there is something you can think of that always makes you laugh or puts you in a good mood. These kinds of activities or experiences are what we're looking for, as long as they can fit within a five minute window.

Here are some example activities you may want to try as a part of your calming routine: sprinting, doing sit ups, dancing or singing to upbeat music, splashing cold water on your face, listening to soothing music, watching a comedian on YouTube, scrolling through your Facebook feed (if you won't get too distracted), pounding your chest to let off some steam, doing a breathing exercise, or doing a muscle relaxation exercise. In general, it makes sense to start your calming routine with something more intense like a sprint, and then winding down to something calm like a breathing exercise or a muscle relaxation exercise.

Choose 3-5 activities and make sure you can complete them all within just five minutes. If you don't feel calmed after trying them out, you can always change your activities. Experimenting with different setups will help you arrive at your ideal calming routine.

A calming routine is meant to be a very quick process to help get your mind back on track. If you have a few extra minutes to spare I think it can be helpful to call a close friend or family member to vent. Just don't let the conversation drag on because the best way to tackle stress is to finish the work that needs to be done.

Remember that the best time to develop your calming routine is *before* a hugely stressful event ever happens. This isn't something you're going to want to figure out during one of your most stressful days.

How Can You Get Your Whole Life into Focus? (Tips #23 - 27)

A truly deep focus is one that isn't easily thrown off track because of random life events. The way to build up your focus to an even deeper level is to determine what your longer-term goals and priorities are. Are your short-term goals part of a larger plan? If your short-term goals don't line up in some way with what you want to do in the long run, then your focus will be limited. In this section you'll learn to take your focus to a higher level by considering where you want to be many years down the road.

#23. Find Your Internal Motivation

Internal motivation is when you want something for its own sake. For example, someone who runs every day probably enjoys running. They may enjoy staying in shape, but they run because they like it, not just to stay in shape. When you have internal motivation, you do something because you like it, not because you expect to get something in return.

How this tip can help improve your focus

Internal motivation is the strongest kind of motivator there is. The more you want to do something without the need for a specific result, the more you'll be able to focus. Think about when you engage with something you really enjoy doing. Perhaps there is a game or hobby you truly enjoy. No one has to tell you to stay focused, right? You do it automatically because it's interesting and fun for you.

It may take some thinking or exploring to discover what truly motivates you, but it will help your productivity immensely if you focus on things you enjoy doing for their own sake. When you know what motivates you, you'll be able to pursue your goals more strongly and focus completely on them.

If you are at odds with yourself, and you work on something with little interest in the task, it will be difficult to focus. Your mind may easily wander to other things you would rather be doing. You can train your focus and work on it, but it will always be dragged down if you don't experience some enjoyment from your tasks.

How to put this tip into action

First, identify your internal motivators. You should list any that you can think of. Even if they're obvious, like spending time with family, it can be helpful to start somewhere.

When you finish with that, think about anything you do in your daily work that you are internally motivated to do. Make sure you think about all of the things you do daily. Consider activities that involve socializing, computer tasks, routine tasks, and any less typical things you may do. You can write them down as well.

If there are parts of your work that you are more internally motivated to do, consider investing more time in those areas if possible. If you do, you will probably find that your focus and performance go up.

If you have no internal motivation in your day to day tasks, it may be time to consider an alternate path. It will be very difficult to focus on your work without having any interest in those tasks. Maintaining a sustained focus will always be an extra challenge if your life is dominated by tasks that you aren't interested in doing.

#24. Know Your Top Three Goals

These are the most important things that you want to accomplish. Think long-term, like in the next five to ten years.

How this tip can help improve your focus

Knowing the top things you want to achieve helps direct your attention where it matters most. Day by day, it's easy to forget why we do the individual tasks we do. It can feel meaningless to check items off of a to-do list if we don't know the greater reason we are completing these tasks. By writing down your top three things, you'll always keep the end goals in sight.

When you have your top three goals decided, you'll be able to keep your focus better. This is because you'll avoid getting distracted by things that don't line up with your main long-term goals in some way. Distractions from our goals are common in everyday life. It's easy to get side tracked with these, but if you know your top three long-term goals, you're much better protected against this problem.

How to put this tip into action

Step 1: Make a list of the most important things you want to achieve, perhaps somewhere from five to ten.

Step 2: Rank the top three most important ones in order, in a new list.

Step 3: If you don't already know how you will accomplish these, you may want to start on action planning (see tip #4) them out to give yourself a more direct route to getting there.

#25. Take Stock of Big Accomplishments

This activity is very simple, easy, and helpful. All you do is take stock of what you've accomplished at the end of the day. Most days, I'll complete one to three key tasks. I have a print-out calendar where all I do is write down in small bullet points the top tasks I completed for the day.

How this tip can help improve your focus

Writing down your big tasks for the day is a great way to make sure you're moving on the right track. Sometimes it's easy to kid ourselves. If you complete ten to-dos for the day, you may feel super productive. But a closer inspection may show that you responded to emails, showed up at a meeting, and went to a dentist appointment, among other low priority tasks. A great way to realistically keep track of whether you stayed focused on important things is to simply write down what you accomplished. The writing on the calendar (or a notebook) doesn't lie.

If you find that you lose focus regularly, and your big daily accomplishments are actually terribly unimpressive, it's a sign that you need to either focus more on important items, reduce distractions, or train yourself to focus better. It's important to monitor your progress in this way so you don't get a false sense of improving your focus when you actually aren't.

How to put this tip into action

This is quite easy. You can use a free print-out calendar from http://print-a-calendar.com, like I did, or you can use a notepad. I like having a printed off calendar because at a glance either I or anyone else can see how my progress is going.

At the end of your work day, simply write your biggest accomplishments for the day. Hopefully you at least accomplished one big worthwhile task. That's actually how I gauge my progress. Did I accomplish something big and important today? One big item is often worth more than ten little ones.

I think it helps to put yourself on the line a bit and leave your calendar in a place anyone can see. You don't necessarily need to go so far as to publish it online, but that might get you interesting results too. If you stray off the path of focus, it's not the worst thing in the world for a friend or spouse to look at your calendar and tell you they think you need to focus more.

#26. Have a Mission Statement

This is a statement that very concisely states who you are, what is most important to you, and what you aim to accomplish in life. In other words, what is your mission?

How this tip can help improve your focus

Having a mission statement helps guide your attention to the most important overall thing in your life. It helps give you a very clear point of focus. Anything that isn't critical to your goals is left out, so you are able to eliminate all distractions and move with complete concentration toward what matters most to you.

One great feature of having such a statement is that any time you're getting off track from your main purpose, looking at your statement will guide you back to where you need to be.

How to put this tip into action

Make a concise statement of your overall focus in life. (Consider the questions 'Who are you?' 'What is most important to you', and 'What do you aim to accomplish in life?')

Think long-term, like a decade into the future or longer. What are you aiming for in that period?

Keep it simple. It should be one or two sentences, ideally.

This is a statement that may change or evolve as you do. Essentially, the point is to sum up who you are, and who you aim to become, all in one or two tight sentences.

#27. Use Reminder Notes and Quotes

These are quotes, questions, and statements that help you remember what your central focus is in life, and why you do what you do.

How this tip can help improve your focus

These notes can help guide your attention to the most important overall thing in your life. Any time you may have doubts or fears creeping up, you can turn to these reminders to get you right back on track.

These notes and messages can also help you remember what inspires you. It can be quite helpful to have a reminder message that is inspiring and directs you along the right path.

As with many other tips in this book, having reminder notes of your main focus can also help you from straying away from your best path and getting distracted with unimportant or irrelevant details.

For example, a couple of quotes and sayings I like are:

"When the going gets tough, the tough get going." - Joseph P. Kennedy (father of John F. Kennedy)

My father sometimes says this. To me, this means that when you're faced with a tough situation, you have to be tough too so you can perform well. If you give up, there's no chance at success.

"You must be the change you wish to see in the world."
- Mahatma Gandhi

I like this saying because we often expect other people to figure out solutions to different problems. The truth is we can start with ourselves.

How to put this tip into action

To develop your own reminder messages, you should keep a log of quotes and sayings that inspire you. Any time you hear or read something that really moves you, it's a good idea to log it so you can read it again later when you need it. If you want to search for helpful quotes, try out BrainyQuote.

The messages you end up using may just be general inspirational quotes, or they may be sayings that are used in your field during difficult periods. They could be wise words a parent or grandparent once said to you. They may even be famous or often quoted words from a leader in your field.

Consider writing or typing some of the most helpful quotes and messages you acquire, and putting them all in one area. You might put them on a page, or perhaps there are posters with some of your messages that you can buy. Either way, it can be helpful to surround yourself with some of these statements in your work space so you can easily have this reminder of where your true focus is. These are all messages that should in some way line up with your top three goals (Tip #24) or with your mission statement (Tip #26).

Make sure you don't forget about your log of inspirational messages. It's good to check back on them periodically, perhaps monthly to make sure you're on the right track.

How Can You Make Sure You Stay Focused? (Tips #28 - 31)

Getting into focus takes time and effort, and it isn't always easy. When you do get there it's a good idea to monitor yourself to make sure you keep a steady focus. This isn't something you need to do every day necessarily, but it's important to do a regular check on yourself to make sure you're moving closer to accomplishing your goals. Sometimes bad habits can creep up on the best of us and bring us back down, so please do not skip this section.

#28. Hold Yourself Accountable

This means having consequences when you lose focus repeatedly.

How this tip can help improve your focus

It can be difficult to get rid of bad habits unless we hold ourselves accountable for them. By keeping yourself responsible for your actions, you'll learn that you can't get away with just not focusing, or without at least trying.

A good way to gradually reduce and hopefully eliminate bad focus habits is to have consequences for yourself. The more you hold yourself accountable, the more you'll condition yourself to build up your focus, and get rid of bad habits. Over time, you'll stay on task even on the tough days, because you won't want to face the consequences.

How to put this tip into action

It's important that you don't punish yourself every time you lose focus. Losing focus isn't necessarily the problem, it's how you react to it that can become the problem. The main idea is to hold yourself accountable for controllable choices you make, such as choosing to take an hour break on social media instead of working on a high priority task.

One way to hold yourself accountable is that if you don't hold your focus well enough, you could make yourself do some makeup work at the end of the day to make up for the lost time. This is something I usually hold myself to. Somehow, the thought of having to do extra work later motivates me to get it out of the way early instead.

As I covered in a prior section, distractions are a big problem for keeping focus. It's good to have rules on how to deal with them. If you find yourself routinely getting distracted by one thing, you might want to place a ban on whatever that big distracter is for 24 hours. I often find that the more I allow myself to play an addictive game, the more I want to play it. If I don't allow myself to play it for some period, I'll often start to lose interest in it and focus more on my work.

Another helpful method I use to hold myself accountable is to use some kind of social pressure. If you have a close family member, friend, or spouse, perhaps they can ask you how well you stayed focused on any given day. Or they could ask you how your progress on your work is going. Often, those two are closely related. This way, if you don't stay focused you need to tell someone about it. It isn't pleasant, so this is a way of holding yourself accountable for your focus habits. This tip can also help you realize if some strategies are especially useful or not useful for holding your focus. For example, your friend or family member may help you see patterns that you missed. Perhaps one of them notices that you never perform well on Fridays, when everyone at the office is chatty because the weekend is near. That might be a good day to bring noise cancellation headphones.

#29. Use a Reward System

Rewards are something positive you get for meeting a focus goal.

How this tip can help improve your focus

Rewards are quite useful because they can help give you motivation to focus more. Most people respond to rewards. Although they are external motivators and not as powerful as internal motivators (Tip #23), they can be useful in small doses.

With rewards, you will be motivated to focus because you'll presumably want to earn more and more of them. I think of them as a way to guide myself in the right direction. But to fixate too strongly on the rewards themselves can be a mistake, as it misses the point. The point of course is to focus your life in the direction you want it to go.

By using rewards you will hopefully condition yourself into a pattern of focusing. The behavior will become more automatic, as you'll get used to gaining rewards for maintaining good focus levels.

How to put this tip into action

There are many different ways you can reward yourself for keeping your focus. I recommend using just a few rewards occasionally.

If you kept your focus through the day and accomplished your key tasks, then it may be a good idea to give yourself some time to relax at the end of the day. You could take work off of your mind and allow yourself to do something pleasant.

You may choose to have a favorite snack, play a video game, or listen to your favorite music. Anything that feels pleasant would be a good idea to try. Find something that you would look forward to doing as you focus on your work through the day. Use that as a reward for yourself on the days you successfully focus.

#30. Seek Mentors

Mentors are people who know much more than you and who can help direct your attention toward what is really important. They can evaluate your strengths and weaknesses and tell you where you should put more of your focus to get the best results.

How this tip can help improve your focus

As you know by now, it's important to know what to focus on as much as knowing what not to focus on. Mentors are a great resource for figuring this out. They've usually done well, so they'll know what is really worth your time and focus and what isn't.

It's important to remember a mentor will usually have been in your place. Even if they were not in your exact position, they've probably had many experiences in your field and they'll generally know what you're going through. Because of this, they're likely to be aware of many common thinking or focus errors you could make. Therefore, they're in a great position to help.

How to put this tip into action

It can be very helpful to find a mentor in your workplace. This doesn't need to be a formal setup. Your mentor could just be a friend at work who has more seniority than you. You could also find a mentor outside of work, perhaps a friend or family member who has been in a similar position as you.

MASTER YOUR FOCUS

It may be useful to ask your mentor to help you guide your attention and focus to what matters most. You could ask them what they think the most important parts of your tasks are, and what the least important parts are. This will help improve your focus and efficiency.

Although it's not the same, you may find forums online of experts that can help you direct your focus as well. There are many forums such as StackExchange, Reddit, and Quora, where experts and amateurs gather to ask and answer questions for each other. These sorts of communities can be a helpful alternative to finding a mentor.

#31. Record Your Time Use

It can sometimes be useful to record what you spend your time on.

How this tip can help improve your focus

It's not always easy to realize just how much time and focus goes wasted. It's so easy to lose focus and have your most productive hours escape you. And yet it is a challenge and takes real effort to focus and keep your attention on the important things in your life. Using a time management app makes it clear just how much time is spent productively, and how much is wasted. In essence, how focused were you?

By seeing where your time has gone clearly laid out in front of you, you're forced to confront the reality of where you put your focus. Perhaps in an eight hour work day you only focused for five or six hours and the rest were wasted. From realizing this, you could make it your goal to focus seven hours and be more productive.

How to put this tip into action

First, I want to mention that this is a tip I don't automatically recommend for everyone. It takes some of your time and focus to be recording your time use accurately all day. However, if you're unhappy with your progress, or if you want to use this as a way to keep yourself accountable, it can be useful for getting your focus back in gear. Personally, I only keep track of my time use if I feel that my focus is off for several days. Everyone has off days, but to have too many of them can be a sign of trouble if you don't do something to fix it.

Now, what is a good way to manage your time? You can use an app like OfficeTime, which can be bought on iPhone, Mac, and Windows. The interface is really nice and makes the process go faster than writing everything out on paper would be. As an alternative, you might try recording your time use in excel or another spreadsheet program.

When you have your program or excel sheet laid out, your next step is to document your actual time use. From the beginning of the day to the end, make sure you record where you spend your time. This may sound daunting, but the OfficeTime app can help make this easier since you can load your most common tasks into it.

Finally, at the end of the day or the week, make sure to look over the results. How can you improve your habits? Did something distract you repeatedly from your goals? Is there something you can change to improve your results? Decide what key changes you need to make, then make them. You can continue to record your time management if you want to keep monitoring your progress.

Final Thoughts (Tips #32 - 33)

You're probably wondering just how fast you can improve your focus. It really depends on how much you work at it, and how seriously you take this. Some people get distracted more easily, and this can make everything more difficult. But determining your weaknesses is an important part of the process.

In fact, if you want to improve your focus fast, you should identify your biggest obstacles or problems to focusing, and start with those. Also, consider where you want to improve your performance the most. For example, if you want to schedule an hour a day to work at home on some art work, then you probably want to make sure you take a break after work to allow yourself to recharge. You also may want to close the door to your room where you work to avoid being distracted by family members. Another example is if you're a big day dreamer, you may want to focus on training your focus (Tips #11 - 18) so you can build up your ability to stay focused on one thing for a longer span. Hopefully this would make you less likely to slip into a day dream.

With that said, I have a couple more tips that I'd like to share with you.

#32. Stay Positive

Don't be too hard on yourself if you lose focus one day. It's good to hold yourself accountable, but making a good effort and trying is a big step in itself. It's a step in the right direction that deserves acknowledgment, even if you aren't able to attain perfect focus.

Just remember that you may sometimes feel like you're falling behind and become disappointed that you're not getting the results you want. However, wallowing in disappointment won't help you focus. If you stay positive you're more likely to stay on track and keep moving forward, making regular progress.

One thing I like to do if I get frustrated by a lack of focus or progress is to allow myself a bigger break than usual. A lot of times I'll come to a new realization during such a break. Sometimes I'll find that a task I was frustrated about can actually be avoided or eliminated in some way. It's not unusual for me to realize that there is a much easier way to tackle a problem than I first thought. Something else I like to do is listen to comedy on Netflix or YouTube. Laughing can help you de-stress, feel positive, and bring your focus back to your important goals.

#33. Practice Your Focus

The whole point of this book is to help you practice your focus. Reading alone won't be enough to take your focus to a higher level. The good thing is you can use a very important tip mentioned earlier in this book to help manage your goals, your time, and your focus. I recommend using that tip, Action Planning (Tip #4), to sketch a plan for how you will improve your focus. I've given many specific examples in this book on how to improve your focus, so hopefully you will use some of them in your action plan. You may also come up with new ideas of your own if you'd like. For example, if you own a board game that requires a lot of focus, that game might make it into being a part of your action plan to improve your focus (even though I didn't mention it).

To make your action plan, make an overall list of the specific tips you want to try. You can start with 5-10 tips from this book to keep it manageable. Then list one or two ways you plan to use that tip in your life over the next month (see 'How to put this tip into action' sections. That's all there is to it. Next month, you could start a new action plan based on how this one goes.

To really make a big change in your ability to focus you'll need to work consistently, but it will pay off in added focus and productivity. Gradually push yourself farther and farther. You might meditate five minutes one day, and ten minutes the next, and so forth. Find your sweet spot of challenge, then push it just a bit further the next day. Stretch your focus. Expand it. The way to do that is to shoot for more and more challenging focus goals.

Favorite Tips

I've personally used, tested and gotten some benefit out of every tip I put in this book. Some of the tips that I've gotten a lot of use from are To-do Lists (Tip #3), Action Plans (Tip #4), Dealing with Disruptive Ideas (Tip #10), Sweet Spot of Challenge (Tip #11), Brute Force Focus (Tip #12), Sustainable Work Hours (Tip #19), Internal Motivation (Tip #23) and Calendar Planning (Tip #25). If you're not sure where to start, then I would recommend some of these because I've found them especially helpful to improving my focus. With that said, all the tips have been helpful to me. I hope you get a lot of use out of them as well.

A Final Reminder

Remember, you're much better off shooting for a sustainable focus than you are a perfect focus. If you can be 90% or more focused, 90% or more of your work time, I think that's a great accomplishment. That's actually what I shoot for. To do that, I usually work around 9-5:30 on weekdays, I'll take Saturdays off, and I'll work at least part of Sundays too. I find that this schedule works for me. It allows me to keep my focus at very high levels, and it allows me to take time to move my body, eat right, and stay energized.

When I work, I don't worry so much about the hours I put in, I just make sure that my focus is in the right place. Of course, I have regular hours, but my point is that I don't measure my productivity in terms of hours spent on a task. I always consider where my focus was, and the quality of work I was able to produce. If I force myself to work much more than I do now, I start to lose energy and focus rapidly. I may work 60 hours and accomplish no more than I would working 40 hours. In fact, the quality of the work is more likely to suffer, and I'll just have to make more corrections later on, delaying my progress.

Sustainable focus is the way to go. You'll be more efficient and ultimately more productive.

Thank You

Thank you for taking the time to read *Master Your Focus*. I hope that you found the information useful. Just remember that a key part of the learning process is putting what you read into practice.

Before you go, I want to invite you to pick up your free copy of *Step Up Your Learning: Free Tools to Learn Almost Anything*. All you have to do is type this link into your browser:

http://bit.ly/Robledo

Also, if you have any questions, comments, or feedback about this book, you can send me a message and I'll get back to you as soon as possible. Please put the title of the book you are commenting on in the subject line. My email address is:

ic.robledo@mentalmax.net

Did You Learn Something New?

If you found value in this book, please review it on Amazon so I can stay focused on writing more great books. Even a short one or two sentences would be helpful.

To go directly to the review page, you may type this into your web browser:

http://hyperurl.co/2imeia

An Invitation to the "Master Your Mind" Community (on Facebook)

I founded a community where we can share advice or tips on our journey to mastering the mind. Whether you want to be a better learner, improve your creativity, get focused, or work on other such goals, this will be a place to find helpful information and a supportive network. I hope you join us and commit to taking your mind to a higher level.

To go directly to the page to join the community, you may type this into your web browser:

http://hyperurl.co/xvbpfc

More Books by I. C. Robledo

Smart Life Book Bundle (Books 1-6) – includes the following:

The Intellectual Toolkit of Geniuses

The Smart Habit Guide

No One Ever Taught Me How to Learn

55 Smart Apps to Level Up Your Brain

Ready, Set, Change

The Secret Principles of Genius

Idea Hacks

Practical Memory

Made in the USA
Lexington, KY
18 March 2018